DIAMOND ELITE

3RD QTR 2018

"A Different Type of Magazine"

Content:

Pg. 2 Mary Kay w/ Atiya McNeal
Pg. 3 Protect Your Ground, Scripts & Beyond
Pg. 4 Battle the Bulge
Pg. 5 SNAP into Entrepreneurialism
Pg. 6 NowWeNo, Leandra McLaurin Coaching
Pg. 7 Kurvy Kouture, Bundles of Pearls, A Touch of Dymples
Pg. 8 Lustful Ladies Boutique
Pg. 9 Paparazzi, Color Me Relaxed, Norma's Bath and Body, Sacred Naturals
Pg. 10 Coretta Campbell, My Addiction
Pg. 11 ENT LLC, Deshonda Jennings
Pg.12 Stiletto K.W.E.E.N of ADHD
Pg. 13 Women's Health Matters
Pg. 14 CBD Oil, Pure Romance
Pg. 15 Mind Body and Soul
Pg. 16 Need A Flyer?
Pg. 17 MakebaDesigns
Pg. 18-22 ambKids
Pg. 23 Cherish
Pg. 24 T&L Stones

Mission Statement:

Diamond Elite Magazine's goal is to boost the exposure and sales of entrepreneurs. We believe networking and word of mouth are the biggest essentials when it comes to small business. As the years continue, we plan to thrive in success and help expand the small businesses who have contributed along the way.

I0498142

Be Sure to Take a Photo and Contact the Small Business Owners/Entrepreneurs directly if you would like to purchase a product or service!

Atiya McNeal
Independent Beauty Consultant

atiyamcneal@marykay.com

(334) 831-7700

www.marykay.com/atiyamcneal

30 FREE FACIALS GIVEN AWAY EVERY MONTH. CONTACT ME FOR YOURS.

One Face. Many Masks.

"Protect Your Ground Personal Safety Products" is devoted to helping "YOU" protect your home, valuables and loved ones against burglary, physical assaults and intruders. You should consider allowing "Protect Your Ground Personal Safety Products" to supply your safety needs because we are your quality self-defense store.

Our product line consists of Batons, Child Safety, Diversion Safes, Jogger/Walker Safety, Pepper Spray, Personal Alarm, Personal Protection, Pet Safety, Safe Family Kits, Safety Lights, and Safety Start-Up Packages, Self Defense, Stun Guns and Survival Gear.

These products are being offered to provide you with a much-needed sense of security for yourself and your family. Purchase knowing that every product is an investment in your personal safety and overall wellness. Buy from a company that you can trust, Protect Your Ground Personal Safety Products.

THAT IS BECAUSE "YOU" DESERVE IT.

www.protectyourground.ecwid.com

Protect Your Ground

www.scriptsandbeyond.com

Scripts & Beyond is a medication review and consulting company, which specializes in providing one-on-one medication therapy management services. All services are provided by pharmacists, who use their clinical expertise to review the current medication regimen, recommend medication alternatives and lifestyle changes, and help create a plan to achieve optimal health outcomes, for each patient. *A Pharmacist Focused On YOU*™ will help provide peace of mind - by ensuring all of the medications and supplements being used are safe, appropriate and cost-effective.

Contact Information

Office Location: 11650 Lantern Road Suite 135 Fishers, IN 46038

Phone: 1- 888-415-0656

Email: info@scriptsandbeyond.com

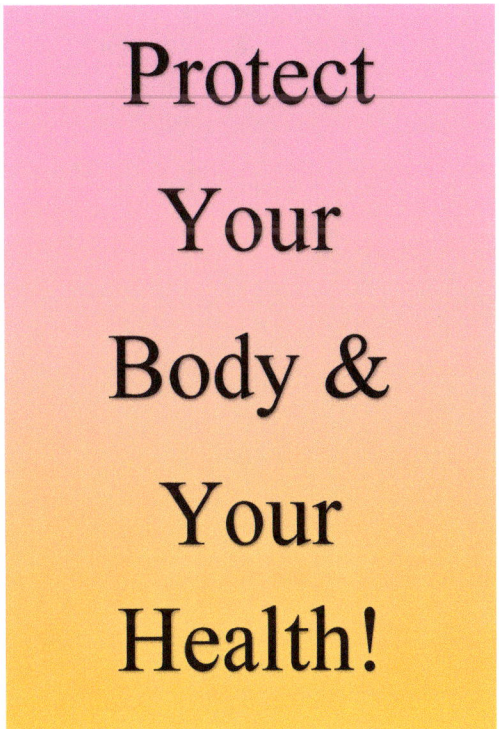

Battle the Bulge

Summertime fun is around the corner! I love having natural energy and keeping my immune system + PH level is balanced.

Did I mention ONE serving of our Greens contains 52 Superfoods and over 16 servings of fruits + veggies?

Who needs to detox?

Ask me how you can receive my 40% discount.

Here are 9 SIGNS Your Body Needs to DETOX:

- Skin breakouts
- Bloating/stomach pains
- Food cravings
- Trouble sleeping
- Constipation
- Headaches
- Fatigue/low energy levels
- Irritability
- Congestion/mucus that feels like a cold!

Call Dee Henry (803) 470-4186 for more information on plant-based products!

www.battlethebulge.myitworks.com

SNAP into Entrepreneurialism
By Victoria Gaskin

You have an idea and want to give this entrepreneur thing a shot. Wonderful! Not to discourage your enthusiasm, but the entrepreneurial world is not missing creativity; it lacks individuals absorbed in implementation.

Being an entrepreneur is not for the faint of heart or those lacking in passion. An entrepreneur is a person who habitually creates and innovates to build something of recognized value around a perceived opportunity. Seemingly, if you have perceived an opportunity to start a business, now you must learn how to create value and launch growth within a previously established market. Undeniably, modern advantages can support almost anyone in this conversion, but even with the best tools at your disposal, you will still be required to work hard. Knowing this, I'd like to share simple elements that will help you SNAP into entrepreneurialism.

S = Share

The adage goes "sharing is caring." I say sharing enriches you with free information. Therefore, why not use your audience of family, peers, and strangers to lobby thoughts around your idea? It's free! Plus, the more you talk about it, the more confident you will become. We'll discuss this in detail later, but try to specifically reach out to individuals currently on the entrepreneurial scene. Doing so will help you build confidence and ensure your efforts are going in the right direction. Most important, while you are sharing, don't forget to include your target market. Your target market is the group of people whose time, attention, and money you will be competing for, therefore include them early. Using the developmental stages of your journey to assess their wants and needs will help you to attract your ideal client.

N = Network

So, what is networking and how do you do it? Simply stated, networking is building specific connections and contacts. An unseasoned entrepreneur may assume to do this you must be invited into large rooms and pass out a handful of business cards. But you don't have to step foot into a room to network. The use of mediums such as chat rooms, social media and groups can immediately connect you with other like-minded visionaries. In doing so, you build relationships and gain business acquaintances for future action. Remember, it's not always what you know but who you know.

A = Advice

Now that you've told everyone who will listen and taken time to connect with like-minded individuals, ask yourself, what have I learned? Information is power and can be empowering to a beginning entrepreneur. And at this point, you should have tons of ideas, suggestions, and materials to rummage through. Designate some time to research the guidance you received and see if it applies to your business idea. All you need is one good piece of advice to avoid an entrepreneurial pitfall and begin a successful journey in business. Keep in mind, if the advice you received doesn't work for where you are or what you're trying to do then don't use it. You can always save it for later.

P = Plan

Planning is where all your efforts will go. In an ideal set-up, a great idea is all you need to experience success in the world of entrepreneurism. However, even the greatest idea, product or service requires a deliberate strategy. What should you plan for? Great question! Your planning for success and preparing for failure. You're developing ways to get the ball rolling and measures to keep it moving in the right direction. You're forecasting instant success and developing how to deal with the long road ahead. Your scheduling sales and market influence and searching ways to raise capital. You must plan for everything. By right, your plan should have a backup plan.

> When you're ready to build a strategy, begin with these:
> - Where's the money coming from?
> - How will I segment my time?
> - What's my marketing strategy?
> - Who can I get to help? And, what specifically can they help with?
> - Who's my target audience?
> - What's my end goal?

Don't be discouraged if you can't answer these questions. I'm merely giving you a great starting point to advance from enthusiasm into action. Like I said, being an entrepreneur will require a lot of work. Hopefully SNAP can motivate you to begin where you are.

> Note: Initially, relying on the internet and technology to network will work fine. But, as time progresses, you should make it a point to attend social functions. My suggestion is to start with one in your local area before tripping across the world. It's not only cost-effective but allows you to impact your local community first. Another win-win for a beginning entrepreneur.

Victoria Gaskin
www.VictoriaGaskin.com
www.BeGre8t.com

According to the Centers for Disease Control and Prevention (CDC) an average of 600,000 hysterectomies are performed on women annually in the United States. This devastating procedure takes away two common bonds that connect women worldwide regardless of race, religion or profession – the hope of motherhood and the desire to have a healthy monthly cycle.

The "Now We No" campaign is an awareness mission highlighting the potentially tragic effects brought about by the misuse of tampons and the overuse of poorly produced sanitary napkins. In this case, what you don't know may harm you. Fortunately, we don't believe in highlighting the problem without presenting a potential solution – Cherish Premium Sanitary Napkins.

Visit www.nowweno.net for more details.

PLACE ORDER HERE: www.cherishmywomb.com

Leandra McLaurin Coaching

www.leandramclaurincoaching.com

Helping women LOVE the skin they're in by healing the relationship between themselves and their body and to show up powerfully in all areas of their lives.

I help women improve their overall well-being by offering support, the right system, accountability and stretching them to reach their full potential.

 @leandramclaurincoaching

 @leandramclaurincoaching

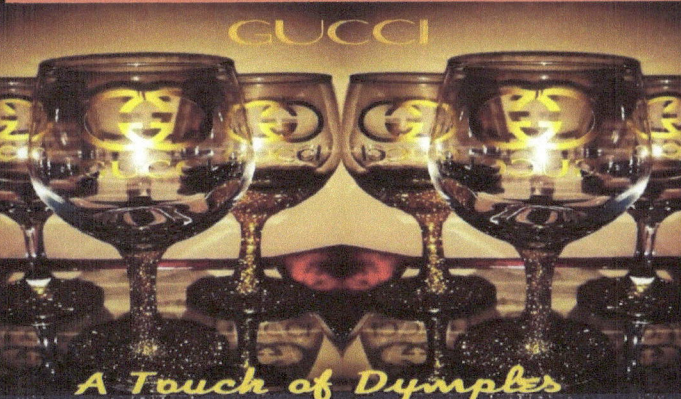

Lustful Ladies Boutique

@lustfulladiesboutique
@lustfulladiesboutique

Lustful Ladies Boutique, LLC offers a wide variety of women's clothing sizes Extra small-5x. We offer cosmetics, jewelry, accessories, handbags, lingerie, and shoes. Feel free to check out our website for exclusive items

MAJOR FASHION STATEMENT!

Annette Chambliss
Independent
Consultant

Email octaviabling@gmail.com
(646) 641-7547

PAPARAZZI
Feed your $5 habit!
https://paparazziaccessories.com/92422

COLOR ME RELAXED

Bringing you an at home spa experience.

Color Me Relaxed offers you a great variety of handmade bath, shower and body products that you can make one-time purchases for or you can commit to one of our monthly subscription boxes.

Boxes are scent themed for a new scent experience every month.

We have something for everyone whether you are a naturalist, prefer only bath, or only shower products we would definitely love to serve you.

www.colormerelaxed.com

Norma's Bath & Body

Welcome to the Body Bakery! Norma's Bath & Body was established in 2004!
Products are perfect for anyone! For women, kids, teens, men, and also a perfect gift for co-workers, nurses, teachers, family as well as yourself! The products are fruity with a variety of delicious scents. Products are available from goats milk glycerin soaps to gift baskets! The lotions are made with Shea Butters, they soften the skin nicely!
Follow Us on FB: Norma's Bath and Body
We Accept Wholesale Orders!

Sacred Naturals

@SacredNatural
@SacredNatural
@SacredNatural

Sacred Naturals sell all Natural Skin Care, Hair Care and Home Products.

www.sacred-naturals.com

Shop w/Coretta Campbell

TRACI LYNN JEWELRY®

Traci Lynn Jewelry

www.tracilynnjewelry.net/3421

BE GLAMOROUS!

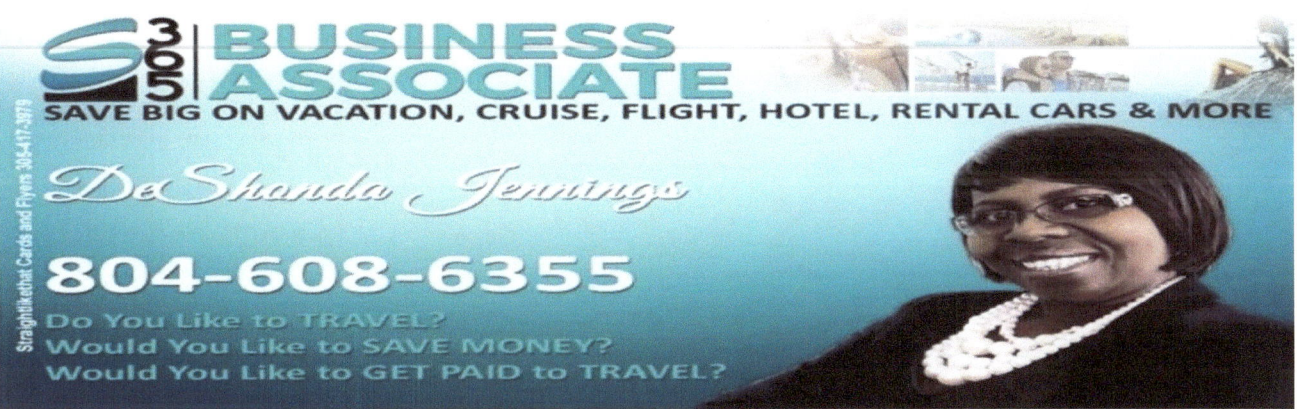

Vacation Packages
www.ytbtravel.com/deejtravel

Stilletto K.W.E.E.N. of ADHD

Voice of Kisha J McRae is known as Stiletto K.W.E.E.N. OF ADHD, Transformation Speaker, and founder of Stiletto K.W.E.E.N. Lifestyle Connections and Facebook community ADHD Stiletto K.W.E.E.N Calm Suite K.W.E.E.N. is an acronym for Kingdom Warrior Eagle Embracing Newer Norms. She is a Mental Illness educator/ambassador, serving kingdom driven moms raising sons 7-16 years of age with ADHD, standing in their Gap Educating other family members about ADHD basics, from 17 year plus personal experience and educational, research and fact standpoint. Helping them to understand their self-care comes first. She helps them develop skills to be a positive support system and work as a unit. She is a parent of a child who is beating ADHD. Not to mention she also has it. Kisha is a 27 year-long Lupus thriver, and an ADHD fighter. Her constant fight with Lupus has made her a Warrior and Advocate for these Mothers to put their mental health and Self-care first. She is a certified Life/transformation Coach with graduating honors from Universal Coach Institute and #1 bestselling author of the book (co-author) "Chocolate & Diamonds of the Woman's Soul and bestselling author of the book walking in my identity, this woman is amazing, and despite illness has continued to obtain many accolades.

"I am a woman she says who at one time, heard God's voice right amid me giving up, memories of being raped, and her lupus diagnosis tormented her, life tried to slay me into an early grave, she expresses." Her family never knew how she emotionally was a wreck. She shares that she is a woman who God gave mercy to even when I refused to listen, hear or serve him." She declares, "He is a merciful God, not to mention almost losing her life with lupus complications." Kisha humbly says, she uses God's promises to "greatly help fuel her faith." In which, His promises are the strength, in any struggle that comes her way. Kisha will tell you with authority that she keeps some of Gods promises in the holster of her heels and have no problem using them as her weapon when the enemy is testing her. Kisha vision is to create relationships with elementary and middle schools parent associations to collaborate and share her story of how she went from victim to becoming a force to be reckoned with in advocating for her son rights and personal and educational needs. **I am Kisha J McRae, Stiletto Kween of ADHD**! Will you share the Krown with me?

The nonprofit, **Nana's Girls' Foundation (NG**F), was formed for the primary purpose of aiding and assisting women in the reinvention of themselves, spiritual development, reeducation, through life coaching and counseling, NGF will offer its clients an opportunity to volunteer with the foundation through our various programs and community events.

These women will receive life skills training, assistance with continuing education, job readiness and search. NGF, Inc. cater to women of all ages. They are required to complete a 6-12 month training program, using the curriculum designed by Dr. Vanessa Williams-Cook, which though designed for all women; caters to the need of each individual person. Upon completion of their individualized training program, each participant will receive a certificate of completion, and assistance with job placement; to include the possibility of working with the foundation in some capacity.

In 2020 NGF, Inc., will open, The Annie Ruth DeLaney Home for Young Women, which will serve women ages 13-40, and provide them with a place of safety, a haven, and home for them if needed. Although not required to live in the home, client will be expected to complete their training program through the home-based program, structure, discipline, and special offerings from the foundation. In 2021, we will open the Genesis Healing for both men and women.

Women's HEALTH MATTERS

INFORM • EMPOWER • INSPIRE

STOP THE SUFFERING IN SILENCE!

IF YOU HAD INFORMATION THAT COULD POSSIBLY SAVE YOUR LIFE OR THE LIFE OF SOMEONE YOU LOVE OR CARE ABOUT, WOULD YOU SHARE IT?

DO YOU OR SOMEONE YOU CARE ABOUT SUFFER WITH SEVERE MENSTRUAL CRAMPS, EXCESSIVE BLEEDING/CLOTTING, FIBROIDS, EMOTIONAL MOOD SWINGS? BATTLE WITH CERVICAL OVARIAN OR BREAST CANCER? EXPERIENCED MISCARRIAGE, REOCCURRING UTI, PID, OR EVEN TSS?

IF YOUR ANSWER IS "YES"
WE HAVE AN EXCLUSIVE PRODUCT THAT HAS LAUNCHED IN THE U.S. AND WILL BE ONE OF THE MOST IMPORTANT MEDICAL BREAKTHROUGHS FOR WOMEN IN THE LAST 20+ YEARS; AND WILL POSITIVELY AFFECT OVER 80% OF THE WOMEN IN THE U.S. AND THE WORLD.

THE "NOWWENO.NET" CAMPAIGN

To Learn More About This Amazing Medical Breakthrough For Women Contact

Diana - 302-766-2281 | Diana@designedbytruth.com
www.Designedbytruth.com
*Distributor Opportunities Available

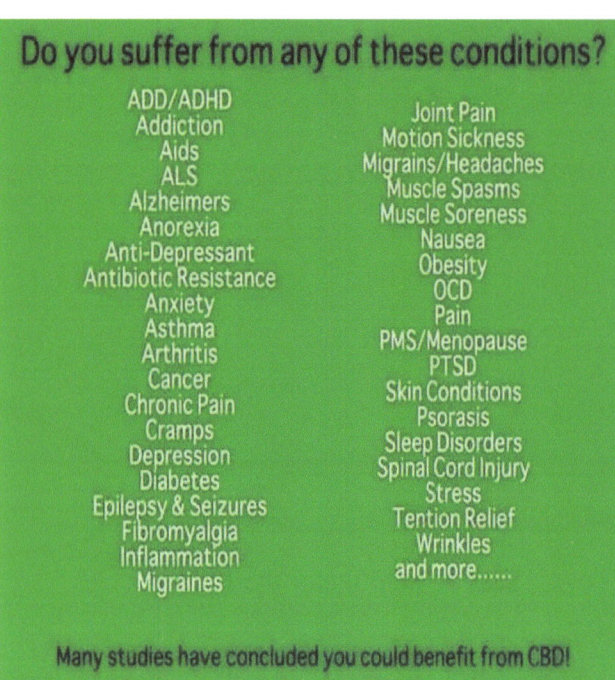

Do Life Different!!
WWW.PRBYEB.COM
Tel: 919-225-9639

Pure Romance by Ebonie

My name is Ebonie, a Director with the company and I am ready to spoil you with some of the best bath, beauty, lingerie, and bedroom accessories around. If you are not ready for a party but would like to get your hands on some of these amazing fragrances, lotions, and lubricants contact me. You can set up a one-on-one shopping experience or shop from my website. If you are looking to add to your income and want to find out more about joining my team, give me a call/text 919-225-9639.

Poetry Corner

Author Mark Edwards

Available at
lulu.com/spotlight/MEdwards1

Poem from
"Afternoon Devotion:
Two Hearts One Soul"

"Mind Body and Soul"

HIM:

Last night I had thoughts about sexing you, loving you... taking off my clothes just to be next to you, then I thought... what a beautiful friend I have in you, so your mind I made love to, your fears I protected you from, your hopes and dreams I combined the two made them into one, made mental notes so one day we can look back and say... we did it all, we been here there and everywhere, no longer hoping and dreaming, just planning the next vacation would be our theme, which Island do you want go to, where you and I could be relaxing, do you prefer the white sands or black sands to tickle your toes, a place where you can lay on your chest, allow me to massage your shoulder blades fingers soothing the pain near your rib cage, let the sun heat you up, as my hands releases just the right amount pressure, I can see your face filled with pleasure, enjoying this soul control as you lay naked, deep in thought as to what's to come next and, wondering should you submit to this grown man's pre-loving, but, what you didn't realize is, I started loving about an hour ago, your mind I enter and kissed, your body I massaged with firm tenderness, and your soul...well your soul I caressed and ask god to bless, keep in mind our love does not have to be perfect, it just has to be true.

HER:

True love is what I always desired, but never acquired, for my mind body and soul was always tired, from the false prophets trying to enter my sensual closet, never taking the time to unlock my mind, indulge in conversation that's sublime, never realizing my mind holds the key to the central city of loving, my internal volcano ready and waiting to explode and release the slow flow of my most sensitive organ, but they didn't know how to talk to me, all they saw was this body's external shell, breast voluptuous hips thick as hell, the aroma that's produced from my skin is emitting sweetest smell, true 4D effect, my body is just a vessel storing organs of intellect, before we can connect, you need to understand why no man was allowed to connect or enter the premises… but, then came you, a man who enter my mind, took your time, made mental love before touching my body, now our body is one as our souls becomes entwined.

Need A Flyer? Contact Us!

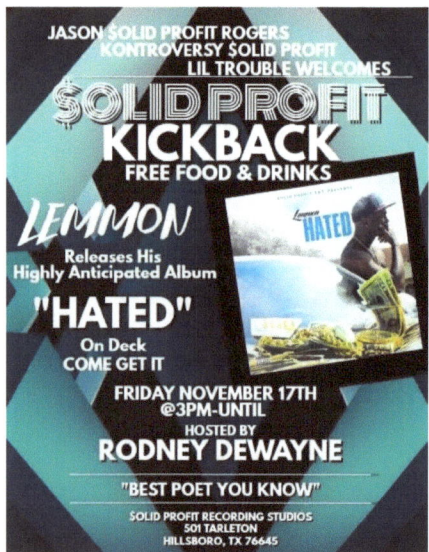

@KandiceSherril

@iKandice

ambKids

ambKids Academy
School of Business

ambKids Academy School of Business supplies students with the life skill training needed for trade specific careers. ambKids Academy School of Business prepares and provides the tools needed to successfully run and develop marketable and profitable businesses.

- School of Product Development
- School of Investments-Real Estate
- School of Publishing
- School of Music Production/Management
- School of Business Development/Management

| Text and Study Skills Books Provided | Self-Paced Studies 3rd-12th grade Level | Great for Classroom Projects and/or Home School Studies | Online study skills support |

ambkidsacademy@gmail.com

Our Mission:

ambKids Academy is an advocacy project with a goal of improving state wide test scores, reading, writing, and life skills training, through learning tool workbooks, publishing books with target messages for youth in areas that will build self-esteem, healthy body image, and social-economic enrichment to better serve the youth in our communities. We have a publishing platform for students, teachers, parents, and professionals interested in writing programs, educational reads, manuals-textbooks. At ambKids Academy we, provide youth with the tools and teaching for entrepreneurship, through training and mentorship. Our mission is to cultivate our cities and towns by coupling enrichment and educational programs to improve the overall sustainability of mental health thus improving morality, grades, and test scores.

AMBKIDS ACADEMY BUSINESS SCHOOL
3RD-12TH GRADES

  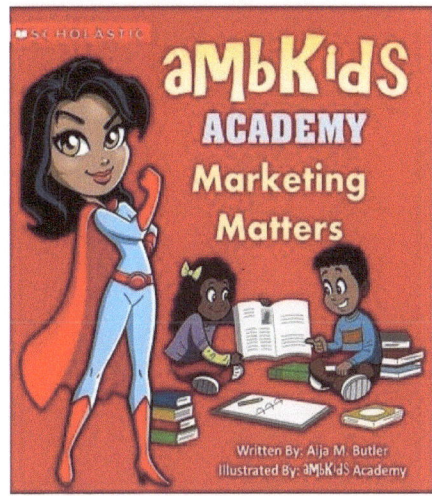

ambKids Academy is an advocacy project with a goal of improving state wide test scores, reading, writing, and life skills training, through learning tool workbooks, publishing books with target messages for youth in areas that will build cognitive development, self-esteem, healthy body image, and social-economic enrichment to better serve the youth in our communities. At ambKids Academy we, provide youth with the tools and teaching for entrepreneurship, through training and mentorship.

Our Project Goal:

- Is to improve reading and writing fundamentals for grades K-12, by providing age appropriate learning tools, launching AMB Junior writer's academy, and providing the necessary training needed to appropriately market and brand ideas founded by our authors, parents, professionals.

- Provide a Publishing platform for young writers age 5-18, parent-child projects, that focus on life skills, reading, writing, math, and entrepreneurial development. • Provide a publishing Platform for Professionals interested in writing text books, self-help, workbooks and memoirs.

- Provide enrichment programs for youth which focus on anti-violence in schools, healthy eating, mental health-self-esteem building, and trade school training.

EDUCATION RESOURCE CENTER CONCEPTS MAY-JUNE RELEASE

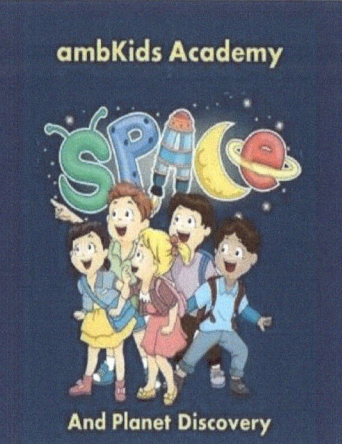

ambKids Academy publishes young authors age 5-17 as well as parent-child projects.

This project developed to encourage school age children to write and use their imagination to create narrative stories, thus increasing cognitive development, social skills, writing and reading improvement, and test scores. ambKids Academy also provides learning tool workbooks for students K-12, which distribute to schools, consumers, and professionals.

Learning Tool Workbooks focus on school curriculum for age appropriate studies, such as, numbers, alphabet, sight words, math, science, and geography. Page 2 Amb Junior writers of America-Publishing house is for authors age 18-21 was developed to teach youth the business of publishing books, writing, marketing, and branding products.

Amb Associated Press, is a coalition of Professionals, Parents, and Teachers with the common goal of improving education with target areas in reading, writing, math, and science, and providing Professional manuals in trade areas of expertise.

ambkidsacademy@gmail.com

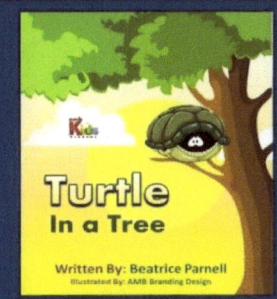
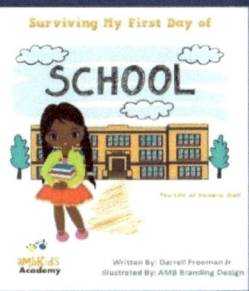
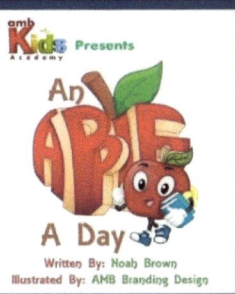
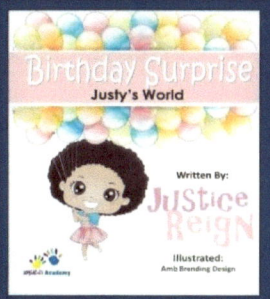
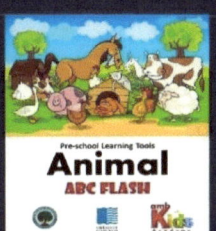
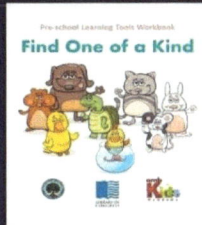
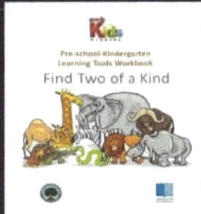
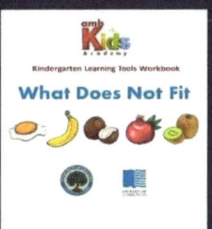
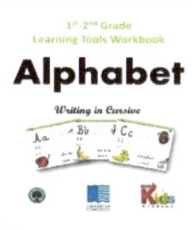
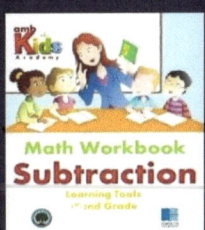
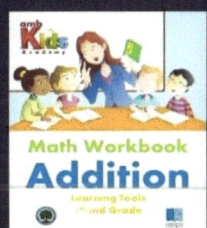
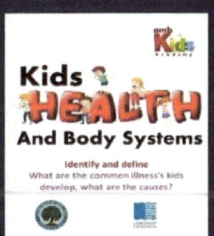
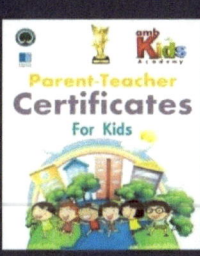

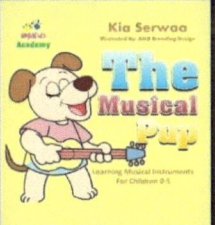
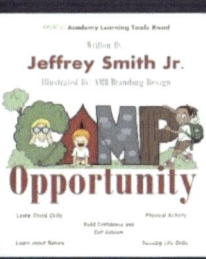
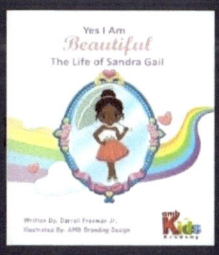
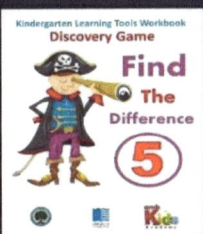
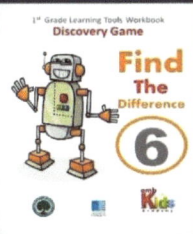
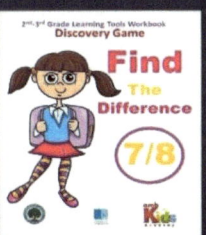

Publications Interest Form:

ambKids Academy is an advocacy project with a goal of improving state wide test scores, reading, writing, and life skills training, through learning tool workbooks, publishing books with target messages for youth in areas that will build self-esteem, healthy body image, and social-economic enrichment to better serve the youth in our communities.

Please Check all that applies:

- ❏ I am a Parent
- ❏ I am an Educator-Teacher
- ❏ I am a Professional
- ❏ I am an Author
- ❏ I am a Student

- ❏ Check here if you are interested in Publishing under ambKids

Enrichment Workbooks and Reads:
- ❏ Self-Esteem
- ❏ Healthy Eating
- ❏ Healthy Body Image
- ❏ Bullying
- ❏ Violence in Schools
- ❏ Social Skill Development
- ❏ Drug and Alcohol Abuse
- ❏ Dating

Science:
- ❏ Biology K-12
- ❏ Anatomy K-12

Math:
- ❏ Addition
- ❏ Subtraction
- ❏ Multiplication
- ❏ Division
- ❏ Fractions
- ❏ Algebra

History:
- ❏ Learning States
- ❏ Learning Continents

English:
- ❏ Spelling Sight Words
- ❏ Reading Age Appropriate

Learning Tools Workbooks:
- ❏ Matching Numbers
- ❏ Abc Flashcards
- ❏ Abc Cursive
- ❏ Colors
- ❏ Telling Time
- ❏ Matching Game
- ❏ Counting
- ❏ Educational Games

Please email us: ambkidsacademy@gmail.com

Cherish
Premium Sanitary Napkins
Love The Way You Feel™

www.deborahsafepads.com

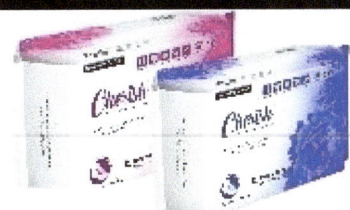  

With Negative Ion Technology

The unique negative ion strip has many proven health benefits including possibly reducing pain and inflammation and may help to neutralize unwanted odors. Now you can maintain an active, carefree lifestyle during that most sensitive time of the month. With Cherish premium pads, you're going to Love the Way You Feel™.

NEED ADVERTISEMENT?

Reach Out By Visiting

www.diamondelitemagazine.com

NEED A HEADSTONE?

T&L STONES 979-217-1795 | WWW.TLSTONES.COM

www.ingramcontent.com/pod-product-compliance
Lightning Source LLC
Chambersburg PA
CBHW051835210526
45473CB00005B/1892